Whispers from Mother Earth

Also by Stella Tomlinson

*Peace Lies Within:
108 ways to tame your mind and connect to inner peace*

Whispers from Mother Earth

Poems and prayers of healing, inspiration and transformation

Stella Tomlinson

Copyright © 2020 Stella Tomlinson

All rights reserved. This book or parts thereof may not be reproduced in any form, stored in any retrieval system, or transmitted in any form by any means — electronic, mechanical, photocopy, recording, or otherwise — without prior written permission of the author.

Visit the author's website at:
stellatomlinson.com

First edition.

Book cover design and internal design by the author.

The Goddess Tree cover image by Pure Design from shutterstock.com

Ancient Spiral Goddess internal image by Bourbon-88 from shutterstock.com

This book is dedicated to Brighid

I am Your Priestess,
And Your flame
is in my heart, always.

CONTENTS

Introduction 1

Opening Prayer..9
Prayer to Mother Earth 11

Whispers from Goddess 13
Introduction 15
I Am 17
The Dance of Life 18
My Sacred Temple 19

Whispers from the Blood & Moon Cycles...21
Introduction 23
Live By The Moon 27
The Call To Bleed 28
Moon Blood 29
Dark Moon Descent 30
Magical Moon.. 31
Moon Whispers 32

Whispers from the Seasons 33
Introduction 35
SPRING: In This Space 37
Emerging 39
Vernal Threshold 40

SUMMER: Beltane Fire 41
Sun Stands Still 42
Lammas-Tide 44
Golden 45
AUTUMN: In The Mother's Garden 46
In The Forest 48
Autumnal Threshold 49
WINTER: Unveiling 50
Descending 51
Stand Still 52
Holding The Opposites 53

Whispers from the Inner Council of Wise Women 55
Introduction 57
MAIDEN: Magical Child 61
LOVER: May-Time Lover 63
MOTHER: Fall Into My Arms 65
QUEEN: Sovereign 68
CRONE: Do Not Be Afraid of The Dark 70

Whispers from the Elements 73
Introduction 75
Dedication to the Mother of the Elements 77
I Am That 78
EARTH: This Body 80
WATER: Blessings of Water 82
FIRE: At Brighid's Forge 83
AIR: I Whisper 84

GODDESS WITHIN: Inner Space 85

Whispers from the Soul 87
Introduction 89

Wise and Loving Soul 91

And Here I Am 92

This Is Life 93

My Soul Sings 94

I Remember 95

The Presence of Love 97

Oh, Let Me Live! 99

Come Back To Your Heart 100

Closing Prayer 103
Our Lady's Prayer 105

What Next? 109

Acknowledgements 111

About the Author 113

Whispers from Mother Earth

Whispers from Mother Earth

Introduction

Mother Earth whispers to us.

Have you heard Her?

She whispers on the wind and through the song of a robin. She whispers through the bloom of a rose and its divine scent. She whispers through sunlight diamonds sparkling on water, and through the roar of the ocean. She whispers through the tender sapling and the gnarled old oak. She whispers through the numinous glow of the full moon and the flow of our menstrual blood.

She is Mother Earth. The Great Mother. Goddess.

She is within you, woman. She whispers through your intuition and flashes of insight and the feeling in your body when something is not quite right.

And She whispers 'yes' to you when you need to make an important decision that may feel scary but also feels very right and true.

She is there in the felt-sense of your joy and love and passion.

I feel Her in the elements that make all of life: earth, water, fire, and air. I feel Her in the moon's ebb and flow, the tides of my menstrual blood, hormones, and emotions, and in the sacred seasons of the year.

And I hear Her whispers guiding me to write.

Sometimes She speaks to me when sitting before my altar in meditation, and I must scrabble for pen and paper to capture the words that arrive fully formed.

Other times, inspiration arrives as I'm gazing at the moon, contemplating a flower or a tree, or when reading. And the words flow through me: prayers, praise, or requests for Her healing love.

So, I share these poems and prayers with you as a gift of the Divine Mother whispering to you, through me. I share them as words of devotion to Her.

I share them with love and trust that in reading them they will touch your soul, as they have touched mine.

Introduction

Do you hear Her? Do you know Her?

Mother Earth. The Divine Mother. Goddess.

For thousands of years She was venerated, as the sacred earth, the source of all life, and the elemental energy that creates, sustains, and ends life.

But the Great Mother largely disappeared from mainstream cultures in the West.

5,000 years of patriarchal religion and culture colonized, demonized, and tried to eradicate the Goddess – yet still She lives on.

You do not have to look far to find Her, for She never truly went away.

She is there in the roots, rocks and soil beneath your feet. In the flow of menstrual blood. She is in the sacred springs and the depths of oceans. She is there in the sunlight and moonlight, in the heat and light of fire, and in the air you breathe.

She is in YOU, in your bones, blood and breath. She whispers to your heart and through your soul. She is in every living thing, in the mineral, plant, animal and human realms.

Whispers from Mother Earth

For She is the life force which will never be quelled. She is Creatrix. She who births, nurtures and destroys. She is the cycle of life.

Feel Her. She is always present, calling you back to Her love.

*

My journey back to Mother Earth – to Goddess – has led me to become Her Priestess, as Priestess of Brighid, She who is Goddess of healing, inspiration and transformation.

You might say the calling began with my birth; that it was in the stars that I would hear the call to become a Priestess of Brighid. I was born at Imbolc-time, on the 2nd of February.

I did not realize the significance of my birthdate until I was in my thirties – when a Pagan yoga teacher friend told me.

This planted a seed, which grew within me and blossomed as a call to live in deep reverence with the cycles of life and the energies of nature, as a daily sacred spiritual practice.

Introduction

And then I felt Glastonbury calling me - the small town in Somerset, in the UK, also known as Avalon. It is a place of profound spiritual connection to the divine feminine and home to the UK's first modern Goddess Temple.

Visiting for the first time in my adult life in 2017 I felt an excited flutter as my husband and I drove there, from our home in Hampshire, and I heard little inner voices trilling "She is coming! She is coming!".

And as I sat in the Glastonbury Goddess Temple for the first time, my whole being relaxed, and my soul felt that I had come home.

Having not even known that there was such a thing as Priestess training, I picked up some leaflets, and within the bunch, was a leaflet about Brighde-Brigantia Priestess training (other names for the Goddess Brighid – She has many!) ... and that little voice within began to call: "what if ...?" "I could do this..." "Yes, I shall!".

And so, it began.

I dedicated as Her Priestess in January 2020. And such a journey it was. Full of love, connection, doubt, frustration, certainty, confusion – and joy!

I wrote many of these poems and prayers in the lead up to and during my two-year Priestess training period, and others since then. Her words keep flowing to me and through me. It's no surprise really – Brighid is Goddess of poets and patroness of Bards after all!

*

So, as you read the poems and prayers in this book, I would love for you to receive the healing and inspiration you need to bring transformation into your life.

The transformation that helps you to discover the light in your heart, the gold in your shadow, and the truth of your soul.

Read them slowly.

Savour them.

Meditate with them.

Receive them.

Introduction

The poems and prayers are presented by themes which reflect different aspects of Goddess:

- **Whispers from Goddess**: these are direct messages from Her to you, through me.
- **Whispers from the Blood & Moon Cycles**: these offer connection to the menstrual cycle and the lunar cycle – the way in which Goddess expresses Herself through our female bodies.
- **Whispers from the Seasons**: these take us on a journey through spring, summer, autumn, and winter as Goddess whispers to us through the ebbing and flowing energies of the wheel of the year.
- **Whispers from the Inner Council of Wise Women**: these offer words of connection to the Maiden, Lover, Mother, Queen and Crone: archetypal faces of Goddess, stages of a woman's life, and wise guardians who live within each of us, always.
- **Whispers from the Elements**: these honour the elements which make all of life: earth, water, fire, air, and spirit.
- **Whispers from the Soul**: these speak to and from the seat of the divine within each of us: the soul. A place of profound wisdom, knowledge and love.

So, this is my hope for you, dear reader.

That you will realize that divinity is not something 'out there'.

Your body is your temple. Your emotions are sacred. Your mind is divine. Your spirit is powerfully aflame.

Mother Earth – Goddess – is within you and all around you.

And She whispers Her blessings to you.

Listen...

With so much love and peaceful blessings, Stella x

A note on terminology

I wish to make it clear that when I use the terms "woman" or "women" in this book that I include all those who identify as being a woman. All gender identities are fully welcomed to read and enjoy this book.

*

I have chosen to capitalize the words Her, She etc. when referring to Goddess.

Opening Prayer

Whispers from Mother Earth

Opening Prayer

Prayer to Mother Earth

When I feel the warmth of Your sun,
May I know I am loved.

When I feel the flow of Your waters,
May I know I am free.

When I feel the protection of Your earth,
May I know I am strong.

When I feel the clarity of Your air,
May I know I am wise.

When I gaze into the beauty of Your rose,
May I know I am divine.

And She whispers:
"Always. Always. Always."

Whispers from Mother Earth

Whispers from Goddess

Whispers from Mother Earth

Introduction

Goddess.

Mother Earth beneath our feet.

The Celtic triple aspect of Maiden, Mother, Crone.

Parvati, Laxmi, Saraswati from Hinduism.

Inanna from ancient Sumer. Isis in Egypt. Astarte from Canaan.

Pachamama from the Inca pantheon.

Mazu. Zhinü from China.

Aphrodite. Artemis. Gaia. Hecate. Just a few of the many Greco-Roman goddesses.

Brighid, Danu, the Cailleach, the Morrigan from the Celtic pantheon.

These are just a handful of names and faces of Goddess through the ages.

She is Mother of the elements: of earth, water, fire, and air. Sun Goddess. Moon Goddess.

She is within all living beings and radiates Her light and love through all of life, and through each of us.

Connecting to Her is really very simple.

She is in all of nature. She IS nature. And as you are a part of nature, Goddess is within you too (whatever your gender).

Let Her re-introduce Herself to you. Let Her envelop you in Her loving presence.

Let the words contained herein bring balm to your soul and soothe your heart.

Open to a profound sense that no matter how desolate you feel that you are never alone.

And in your joys and most blissful moments, here too, you are never alone.

The whole contents of this book you are holding are whispers from Goddess.

But in these first three pieces She is speaking to you directly.

Hear Her words and receive Her love.

I Am

I am the wind that blows through leaves,
I am the power of the seas,
I am the sunlight shining down,
I am the earth that's all around.

I am in the river's flow,
I am above and below,
I am the bird which flies so high,
I am the blue expanse of sky.

I am the roots which burrow down,
I am the strong and stable ground,
I am the silver of the moon,
I am the beauty of flowers' blooms.

I am the flame which burns so bright,
I'm in the dance of fire light,
I am the rain that falls to earth,
I am there at every birth.

I am in every breath you breathe,
I am in all that you perceive,
I am in every stage of life,
I am the soul's midwife.

I am here with you now,
Feel My kiss upon your brow.
And know that we shall never part,
For I am always in your heart.

Whispers from Mother Earth

The Dance of Life

I come to you with each breath you take
Feel Me now in the air you breathe.

Inhale My energy and life,
Sparkling into each cell of your being.

Let Me bring you inspiration
And expansive freedom and oceans of possibilities.

Exhale out to Me your tiredness and frustration and fears,
Release to Me your anger and doubt.
Let them all go,
And fall into My embrace.

Surrender to the flow, to the rise and fall.
Trust in your breath and trust in My presence.

Let Me breathe you into your most radiant fullness
And know that I am always with you.

Feel the dance of your breath, ebbing and flowing,
And let us dance together for eternity, My love.

Whispers from Goddess

My Sacred Temple

Breathe into your belly
Breathe into your womb
Your body is alive woman
It's not your tomb.

Feel your heart beating
Feel your pulse throb
Your body is your home woman
Living is your job.

Sense Me on your inhale
Sense Me breathing out
Your body is My temple woman
Sacred, have no doubt.

So, breathe Me in your belly
Breathe Me in your womb
Feel My power within you woman
And let your soul bloom.

Whispers from Mother Earth

Whispers from the Moon & Blood Cycles

Whispers from Mother Earth

Introduction

Since ancient times, humanity has been drawn to the moon ... and has used its waxing and waning as a guide to living life in flow with the sacred rhythms of nature.

There are numerous Goddesses of the Moon found throughout history across the world.

Here are just a few of them.

Aine: Celtic Goddess of the Moon and the Sun.
Artemis: Greek Goddess of the Moon and of the hunt.
Arianrhod: Celtic Goddess of the Moon and stars, her name means 'Silver Wheel'.
Ceridwen: Celtic Goddess associated with the waning Moon.
Chang'e: Chinese Goddess of the Moon.
Juna: Roman Goddess of the New Moon.
Luna: Roman Goddess of the Moon, the words 'lunar' and 'lunatic' derive from her.
Selene: Greek Goddess of the Moon, particularly associated with the full Moon - and from whom the word Selenophile derives, meaning 'moon lover'.
Zirna: Etruscan Goddess associated with the waxing Moon.

The moon has long been associated with the feminine aspect in nature: the cycles of life and death and rebirth and the monthly rhythm of the menstrual cycle, as well as with intuition and introversion and the deep tides of emotion we feel as human beings.

But in 21st century life, we're constantly pushed to strive and achieve and grow; to be outgoing and always be team players. Extroversion is lauded and introversion is scorned.

We're taught that emotions are messy and should be pushed down. We've been programmed to believe that intuition shouldn't be trusted – that it's just a figment of our imagination. Ancient traditions and beliefs and ways of healing are banned, derided or labelled 'old wives' tales'.

We're taught to ignore the menstrual cycle and be consistently productive and active, no matter where we are in our cycle. There is no room for the fact that people who menstruate experience peaks and troughs of energy and emotions throughout each month.

Whispers from the Moon & Blood Cycles

Mainstream culture would look askance at the suggestion that there is a link between the moon, emotions and the menstrual cycle.

Yet the moon shifts huge bodies of water through its effect on the tides. Why wouldn't this affect us? We humans, who are around 60% water?

The luminous moon is there in the sky above, waxing and waning through every month, showing us that it is natural to ebb and flow.

The moon reminds us there is another way to live.

The moon guides us to reclaim what we feel in our bones and in our blood.

She reminds us that life moves in cycles. She guides us to look within and reconnect to the wisdom of our intuitive bodies.

The moon reminds us that it's natural to have peaks and troughs of energy; to have periods of growth and periods of falling away; to shine brightly and be out in the world sometimes, and she teaches us to accept that it's OK to turn away from the world and look within too.

The moon calls us back to our true self that is one with nature.

As women, we embody the cycle of life.

It's in the monthly blood cycle; the waxing and waning of our energies and emotions.

The waxing moon energy of pre-ovulation; the full moon energy of ovulation; the waning moon energy of pre-menstruum; and the dark/new moon energy, embodying the simultaneous death of the old cycle and beginning of the new, with the arrival of blood and menstruation.

But if you don't menstruate, you may wish to tune into these energies through the journey of the moon herself each month and notice if and how your inner world attunes with her monthly dance.

Honour the whispers of the Goddess through the moon and your blood cycles – and reclaim your connection to the mysteries of life.

Whispers from the Moon & Blood Cycles

Live By The Moon

Dark moon calls me
Deep, deep within.

New moon shows me
It's time to begin.

Waxing moon leads me
To grow and shine bright.

Full moon fills me
With love and delight.

Waning moon invites me
To trust and let go.

'Til dark moon reclaims me
To the temple below.

Lady Moon guides me to wax and to wane
To live in rhythm and become whole again.

The Call To Bleed

Descending. Sinking.
Parting. Leaving.
The inner temple is calling me to come.

Calling me to set aside the worldly life
And go within.

To dream, to feel, to understand.
To be open to it all.

Inhabiting and embracing the darkness.
Warm and pulsating and nurturing.
Deep and dark and red.

The inner temple is calling me
To listen to and heed my blood wisdom.

Inner sight: clear seeing.
Inner voice: clear hearing.
Inner senses: clear feeling.
Inner knowledge: clear knowing.

The birthright of woman.

Whispers from the Moon & Blood Cycles

Moon Blood

In the darkness of the moon,
In the rich redness of my blood:
There lies my deepest wisdom.

Ancient knowing.
Infinite insight.

Guided by my blood wisdom,
I look within.

I embrace the darkness and close my eyes to distraction.

And I feel the truth in my womb and Her blood and Her wisdom.

I know.

Dark Moon Descent

Dark moon
Womb tomb
Where life ends and begins.

Blood red
Death black
I soften with relief.

Held close
Secure within
Suspended in viscous blood.

Blessèd stillness
Sacred silence
I yield to my deaths.

Release, surrender
Dissolve, destroy
All I once held fast.

Memory fades
Time slides
I sleep within your depths.

Dark moon
Tomb womb
I trust in my rebirth.

Magical Moon

Magical moon, shine your mysterious light into my heart.
Soothe my mind,
Opening it to the mysteries of life.

Magical moon, your glow flows into and through me.
Silvery, mystical.
Subtle and shimmering.
Ancient. Constant.

Magical moon shadows enchant me.
Your waxing and waning ebbs and flows with my blood.

I am compelled to gaze upon your light,
And your generous loving glow.

Magical moonlight shines through my soul.

Whispers from Mother Earth

Moon Whispers

I am Luna
Silver light on your brow.

Shining mystery.
Calling you to Me.

To the liminal spaces
In between past and possibility.

The truth of your soul, illuminated.

I know you feel My call.
You are My Priestess.
Open your heart, your mind, your vision
And I will show you all of time.

Gaze upon My face
As your ancestresses have always done.
And know you are one and all together,
For eternity.

This is my promise to you.
Listen. Listen. Listen
To My silver whispers,
Calling you home.

*

*Written at Lunar Imbolc:
the full moon in February 2020*

Whispers from the Seasons

Whispers from Mother Earth

Introduction

The seasons of the year, as they wax and wane, feel like Mother Earth breathing.

Her inhale of spring and summer lasts six months and Her exhale of autumn and winter lasts another six months.

This is the natural rhythm of the year. Inhale and exhale. Rebirth and growth followed by releasing and death. This is the cycle of life.

In this cycle of life there is no beginning and no end. It is an ever-moving turning. All unfolding as it should. The turning of the Moon around the Earth, and the Earth around the Sun. A mysterious intelligence keeps it all in flow, in synchronicity.

This turning is embodied in the eight festivals of the Celtic Wheel of the Year. These are ancient festivals and remembrances which connect us to our pre-Christian ancestors.

They are: Spring Equinox (day and night are of equal length), Summer Solstice (longest day), Autumn Equinox (day and night are of equal length) and Winter Solstice (shortest day).

Then we have the four Celtic Fire Festivals that are cross-points between the solstices and equinoxes and relate to the agrarian calendar and the changing of the seasons, but also to life's phases.

These are: Imbolc (early spring, the awakening of the land, and childhood), Beltane (fertilization of the land and young adulthood), Lammas (abundance of the land, first harvest, and our creative years) and Samhain (final harvest, the apparently dead land, and older age and preparation for death).

Develop a relationship with the seasons as they change around you.

Notice the new life, hope, and inspiration of spring; the growth and fullness of summer; the releasing and letting go of autumn; and the stillness, clarity, and restfulness of winter.

They each have their own unique gifts for your body and soul.

Remember, that you are a child of nature – of Mother Earth.

Let Her flow bring you back to wholeness.

Whispers from the Seasons

SPRING

In This Space

Bare branches, against a bright, blue sky.
Sap is rising, yet I will wait awhile.

Spring is coming yet I am happy at the cusp,
Knowing life is reawakening but I don't need to rush.

Here in this liminal space, as the wheel turns,
I find myself resisting the fire which is ready to burn.

"Slow down, no rush, all in good time"
A voice within my soul whispers, "to yourself, be kind".

"Here in this space between winter and spring
Connect with the joy the inner child can bring.

"Be silly, be vibrant, enjoy life and play.
The time to birth dreams will soon have its day".

These words arrive, fully formed, in my heart.

Thank You blessed Lady
For the wisdom You impart.

Emerging

Life is stirring, rising, reawakening.
The long winter is coming to an end.

Green shoots burst forth, courageously inching into the fresh, cold air.

Birds begin to sing their dawn callings, feeling warmer days are on their way.

Snowdrops dance their pure, white radiance against the still, bare earth.

The slowly strengthening sun calls forth new life.

The dark womb of winter has nurtured me, held me ... but now I am ready to re-emerge.

Reawakening to hope and anticipation.
Energy rising. Eyes opening.
Arms expanding. Inner fire growing.
Tender heart radiating love and joy.

The nascent spring and its blessings beckon me.

And I emerge to embrace this miraculous, mysterious life.

Vernal Threshold: A poem for the Spring Equinox

Poised at this moment of perfect balance,
Time stops as I close my eyes.
Behind me the darkness of winter is fading,
Before me, the brightness of spring calls me on.

The cocoon of winter held me safe in its depths
And I yearn to stay in its magic and dreams,
Yet something inside me is stirring and rising
To step forward and blossom and bloom and trust.

So I turn to the sun and its warmth bathes my body
I feel taller and stronger and ready to grow,
I step over the threshold into spring-time's unfurling
With a heart filled with joy at the beauty to come.

Whispers from the Seasons

SUMMER

Beltane Fire

Beltane fire burns bright within me
Beltane fire of magic and truth.

The fire of courage glows within me
The fire of passion and fertile youth.

To jump the fire, I summon courage within me
To jump the fire, in my strength I trust.

Leaving behind all that restrains me
Leaving behind self-doubt and mistrust.

I jump the fire, its flames transform me
I jump the fire, into the light.

I land, and limitless joy flows through me.
I land, and my radiant spirit shines bright.

Sun Stands Still: A poem for the Summer Solstice

Sun stands still.
And I feel the light shining into my mind
Bringing with it the potential for deep clarity and the most vivid illumination.

Sun stands still.
And I feel the pause in time ...
Slowing down into perfect stillness.
Expanding into freedom.
Infinity within me and around me.

Sun stands still.
And I sense the sweetest healing waters washing through me,
Cleansing my worry, doubt and fear,
Sparkling in the sunlight; diamonds in the flow.

Sun stands still.
And I feel my deep and tender heart within me
Full of love and wisdom and insight, ready to be shared.

Sun stands still.
And I open to the stillness;
Yield to the pause …
Listen for guidance and take comfort from the reflections which arise.

Sun stands still.
And I breathe.
I pause. I reflect …

As the wheel soon turns again.

Lammas-Tide

Golden abundance...
Juicy, ripe fullness.

Infinite love...
Swells and flows and fills me up.

My heart expands with gratitude...
And bursts into golden light.

Enough to fill the universe.

Golden

Leaf of green.
Leaf of gold.

Lit up within by light
Shimmering and pulsating into and through each vein and cell.

Miraculous with life.
Knowing when to grow and when to die and when to be reborn.

The light and life which energizes every cell with divine love
Fills my heart with the same golden pulsating fullness.

I am overwhelmed with love:
The love that is life.

And my heart shines...

Golden.

Whispers from Mother Earth

AUTUMN

In The Mother's Garden

In the Mother's garden
Ripe apples are in abundance
Hanging from the branches in rosy, sweet-scented fullness.

In the Mother's garden
Are juicy berries and currants and fruits galore
Full of taste and life: a feast for the senses.

In the Mother's garden
Is nurture and plenty and unconditional love
As She gives and gives of Her abundance
Without expectation or demand.

In the Mother's garden
We see the circle of life –
Birth, growing, blooming, fruiting, giving, and dying…
And the cycle begins again.

In the Mother's garden
Is life itself

And all that I need and more.

I offer my blessings to the Divine Mother of us all
For the unceasing abundant love She offers Her children.

*

*Written in the Orchard of Avalon,
in Glastonbury Abbey grounds,
September 2018*

In The Forest

Quiet, damp, fullness surrounds me.
Soft underfoot, protected above.

Stillness. Expectation.
Feeling unseen eyes watching.

Fresh, sharp-clean air at my nostrils.
Vibrant life filling my lungs with each breath.

Joy.
Such deep contentment.

The trees welcome me.
I have come home.

Whispers from the Seasons

Autumnal Threshold: A poem for the Autumn Equinox

Poised at this moment of perfect balance,
Time stops as I close my eyes.
Behind me the brightness of summer is fading,
Before me, the darkness of winter beckons me on.

The joy of summer enlivened my soul
And I yearn to stay with its magic and life.
Yet something inside me calls me to settle
To rest and surrender, to slow down and trust.

So I lie on the earth and Her strength holds my body
I feel safe and protected and ready to dream,
I step over the threshold into autumn's releasing
With a heart filled with faith at the transformation to come.

WINTER

Unveiling

Feeling untethered, yet so very grounded.
Feeling lost, yet safely on my way home.

Knowing all is shifting, yet feeling balanced.
Needing company, but being content on my own.

Falling into the dark depths of winter,
Shedding, releasing ... I know not what.

Falling apart. Falling into freedom.
Disruption, I sense, will play its part.

All these feelings, I welcome into me
As Samhain's unveiling reveals the depths.

A beautiful, welcome, and unshakeable certainty that all is changing,
Into my heart has crept.

Descending

No words. Just feeling.
Drawing in, releasing.

Going inwards – a natural calling.
Moving into the dark – the nurturing womb of winter.

Looking within. Reflecting.
Time to dream, no need for action.

Quietening.
Softening.
Slowing.
Just being.

Descending into the cave of my heart.

Laying myself down to rest 'til the light is returning.

Stand Still: A poem for the Winter Solstice

Stand still. Close your eyes.
Breathe. Quieten the mind's churning.

Stand still. Look back at your year.
What is its learning?

Stand still. Look within,
And feel for what you are most yearning.

Stand still. Light the solstice flame.
See it burning.

Stand still. Feel the joy,
For the light is soon returning.

Get ready to move.
For the wheel of life is ever turning.

Holding The Opposites

Feeling pulled into bleakness.
Somehow comforting ... so familiar.
A blanket of muffled oblivion.

It would be so easy just to slide down underneath it and disappear into its welcoming, nihilistic blackness...

But... It's a false promise of comfort.

Yes, it would be easy to slip into oblivion.
But the life force in me stirs and says "no!".
It says, "don't fall into 'no'".

So, what can I say yes to instead?

Yes, to the sunlight glowing on bare branches in my garden.
Yes, to the waxing moon glowing in the daytime sun-lit sky.
Yes, to snowdrops.
Yes, to life returning.
Yes, to life is confusing and painful ...
And yes, to living it anyway.

And when 'no' begins to creep into my bones once again ...
I shall ask my bones to sing their 'yes'!

Whispers from Mother Earth

Whispers from the Inner Council of Wise Women

Introduction

Our Celtic ancestors saw the Earth as the manifestation of a triple-aspect Goddess.

The Maiden Goddess of spring and the waxing moon; the Mother Goddess of summer and the abundance of early autumn, and the full moon; and the Crone Goddess of winter and the waning moon.

This triple deity is found all over the world.

And it easily maps to the stages of a woman's life. Maiden – Mother – Crone.

In more recent years, this has been expanded: often an additional aspect of 'Enchantress' or 'Wild Woman' is added between Mother and Crone.

However, as I was taught in my Priestess training, I work with these five aspects:

Maiden – Lover – Mother – Queen – Crone

This reflects a greater complexity of the stages of a woman's life.

And it reflects that we live longer than we used to!

Of course, there are many more archetypes, energies and facets to life, and of a woman's psyche, than just these five.

But I feel that this expansion of the traditional triple aspect of Goddess offers us a useful way to connect to different parts and potentialities within ourselves.

For no matter your age, all these energies and archetypes exist within you. They are potential energies which exist out of time, whether you have experienced that stage of life or not. They are faces of the Goddess within *you*.

They are your inner council of wise women. Here to inspire, protect and nurture you.

Inner Maiden – She is the magical child within of joy, lightness, hope and curiosity. She is innocent and playful and open to new experience. Life is a delightful and fun game to Her!

Inner Lover – She who is full of passion, sensuality, courage and limitless love. She embraces all that life has to offer. She is independent and free. She is a woman unto Herself and fearlessly equal in any partnership.

Whispers from the Inner Council of Wise Women

Inner Mother – She who loves you unconditionally no matter what. She is always there for you, cherishing you and supporting you on your path.

Inner Queen – She who is sovereign of Her realm. She has clear boundaries which She communicates with a strong presence. She is just and fair but has zero-tolerance for nonsense and ignorance.

Inner Crone – She who is ancient and wise. Drawing deeply from the well of knowledge gained through Her experience, She sees the truth, and knows just what you need to do or say. She has seen it all! She may appear fearsome for She is the bringer of death, but do not be afraid, for death is a natural part of the cycle of life.

Call on their magic, wisdom and love!

Whispers from Mother Earth

Whispers from the Inner Council of Wise Women

MAIDEN

Magical Child

Magical child with sparkling eyes
And laughter like diamonds,
You dance with life.

Magical child you are the light
Of hope and innocence,
Your soul shines bright.

Magical child of joy and fun
Life's your adventure,
And the game's just begun.

Oh, I remember your world of fairies,
Of mystery and magic,
So enchanted and merry.

I remember that I once was you,
Playful and hopeful,
Trusting and true.

And you are still with me, in my heart,
We travel together,
We will never part.

Whispers from Mother Earth

Oh, magical child within my soul
I love you dearly
I hold you close.

So, magical child, let's have fun and play!
Let's ride your unicorn,
And embrace today!

Magical child with our sparkling eyes
With laughter like diamonds,
We shine through life.

Whispers from the Inner Council of Wise Women

LOVER

May-Time Lover

Sensual, sexual, wild and free,
Lover Bride, She beckons me.

Blossoming, blooming, alive at last
Now that the dormant time of winter has passed.

Courageous, fearless, strong, and true,
Can you hear Her calling you?

"Rise up in love, dear radiant soul,
Live from your heart: courageous and bold.

"Dance off the shackles of fear and doubt,
Speak your truth, clear and loud.

"Breathe deeply and feel the flame within.
Jump the fire; it's time to begin

"To live your life with passion and fun,
Leave behind the fears, lift your heart to the sun."

Stand strong in your power, firm and true,

Let Lover Bride shower Her blessings on you

Of passion and power, self-acceptance and love,
And embrace all that you are and all that you've done,

And all that's within you, ready to shine,
For you are beauty. You are divine.

*

'Bride' is the name for Goddess Brighid in Her Lover aspect, associated most strongly with Beltane – but She's always with you!

Whispers from the Inner Council of Wise Women

MOTHER

Fall Into My Arms

It's okay...
Rest awhile here in My arms.
It's okay...
Let Me keep you safe from harm.

It's okay...
You didn't do anything wrong.
It's okay...
I've been with you all along.

It's okay...
Feel My kiss upon your brow.
It's okay...
For I am here with you now.

It's okay...
Just let your body breathe.
It's okay...
I'll give you all the love you need.

It's okay...
Let your fears fall away.
It's okay...
In My arms you can stay.

Whispers from Mother Earth

It's okay...
Tears are healing water.
It's okay...
You are My beloved daughter.

It's okay...
I've been with you all your life.
It's okay...
I've seen the tears and strife.

It's okay...
I know you're grieving and in pain.
It's okay...
Let My presence take the strain.

It's okay...
To feel lost and confused.
It's okay...
For with My love you are imbued.

It's okay...
I love you, dearest one.
It's okay...
Let all your cares be gone.

It's okay...
I see the beauty in your heart.
It's okay...
Trust that we will never part.

It's okay...
All your parts make you whole.

Whispers from the Inner Council of Wise Women

It's okay...
The world needs your gifts and soul.

It's okay...
You are heard and seen by Me.
It's okay...
Be yourself. Radiant, strong, and free.

Whispers from Mother Earth

QUEEN

Sovereign

Queen Goddess of Earth, strong and true,
I need You now: I call on You.

Protect me with Your fearless presence,
Help me embody Your divine essence,

To face my fears with courage in my heart;
Standing tall, with Your ever-present support.

With roots connecting me to Your nurturing trees,
I accept the past, now it's time to release.

And this I proclaim for all to hear:
I am Queen of my realm; my boundaries are clear.

In this realm there is no judgment or cruelty,
This realm is filled with Your love, joy and beauty.

I stand here now in presence and grace

With strength and clarity, the future I embrace.

Now I reclaim my power to feel safe, healthy and whole
And to live from my heart and my radiant soul.

Whispers from Mother Earth

CRONE

Do Not Be Afraid of The Dark

I feel Her calling me.
Her wizened, wise finger beckoning me into the darkness.
I feel afraid, for I fear what lies there in that velvet shadowy blackness.
Yet I yearn for rest and stillness,
So, the longing outweighs the fear,
And I close my eyes.

The darkness enfolds me
And She is there.
The Dark, Ancient Mother, with the wisdom of ages in Her bones.
Fiercely loving.
She calls me on.
And I sink deeper and deeper into this womb of darkness.
I am safe and held in its inviting embrace.

"Do not be afraid of the dark, My love,
For here lies your deepest wisdom, your innermost knowing and truest guidance.
Rest awhile My beloved.

Feel and listen and know in this black stillness.
There is nothing to fear here.
Breathe and let go.
Release the old wounds and hurts and patterns.
Take your time.
I see you in your fearlessness and beauty and wisdom.
Let Me be with you and within you.
And in good time, you shall be ready to be reborn."

And so, I surrender to this darkness, with blessèd relief.
I feel Her mantle enfolding me.
I come to rest, and my soul's yearning is fulfilled.

Do not be afraid of the dark, my love,
For here lies your birthright, your deepest blessings and the wisdom of your soul.

Whispers from Mother Earth

Whispers from the Elements

Whispers from Mother Earth

Introduction

Let us now connect to the sacred elements of Mother Earth.

To Her earth, water, fire and air – which then combine as spirit and the Goddess within.

The four elements are the most tangible way we can feel Her presence.

Through the earth beneath your feet you can connect to Her nurturing protection, strength and abundance – and remind yourself that you have these qualities within you, guiding you to be present in your body.

Her earth is in your body: your bones, muscles and sinews.

Through the waters of life, you can connect to Her flow and depth, to Her healing and cleansing – and remind yourself that you have these energies available to you always, balancing your emotions.

Her waters are in the flow of your emotions and your menstrual blood or in the energy of the womb space.

Through fire invite Her warmth and passion into your life, and the gift of transformation and courage – and remind yourself that these are available to you, always, enlivening your spirit.

Her fire is in your spirit: aflame with passion and vibrant energy.

Through the air dancing around you, connect to spacious freedom, to clarity and insight, and the song of the soul – and remind yourself that with each breath you take, these energies flow through you, clearing your mind of debris.

Her air is your breath: the source of life and the space between the thoughts.

Connect to Her elements for the deepest healing and feeling of belonging to the web of life.

And as you are made of these elements, know that Goddess is within you, always.

Dedication to the Mother of the Elements

My body is Your earth, and You and I are one.

My blood is Your water, and You and I are one.

My breath is Your air, and You and I are one.

My spirit is Your fire, and You and I are one.

And my heart is Your heart, beating together for all of time.

For You and I are one.

I Am That

I am the roots
That delve deep into the earth
And the life energy that rises through them.

I am the gently flowing stream
And the impossible strength of the ocean:
Unstoppable.

I am the fire that burns and warms
And destroys and transforms:
The perpetual flame burns within you.

I am the air which dance around us
The air which brings life
And ideas and inspiration and words to move.

I am ether and space: free, formless,
Mysterious, timeless,
Unknowable and all-knowing.

I am the life force
That blesses all living things.
I am the spirit
That weaves through us all.

I am rooted and flowing, fiery and inspired,
Free and all-seeing,
Wise and connected.

Life flows through Me.

I am that
That I am.

EARTH

This Body

This body is sacred.
The bones, the flesh, the blood.
Its strength and stillness,
Its movement and balance,
Its intelligence – sacred and divine.

This body is sacred.
Its wings and feathers and beaks.
The magical ability to fly,
Rising on the air and soaring through the sky,
Knowing precisely where to go.

This body is sacred.
The roots and branches
Veins, buds, and flowers.
Every cell filled with knowledge
Of life unfurling with divine timing.

This body is sacred.
The stones and the rocks and the crystals.
The mud and earth and soil.
The grass and weeds and flowers.

All in its rightful place and living in its own space.

This body is sacred.
The rivers and valleys and mountains.
The fields and streams and hedgerows.
The forests and woodlands and glades.
The deserts. The oceans. The continents.
Our habitat.
Our home.

And in your sacred body every cell is filled with light and love
Within and around and between.
It offers you a home to the divine:
Embodiment in earth and water, fire and air, and in flesh and bone.

Billions of individual bodies
Forming the body of life.

And this body is blessed and whole and beautiful.

This body is sacred.

Whispers from Mother Earth

WATER

Blessings of Water

Goddess of Water
May Your still, sun-lit, moon-reflecting waters
Bring the healing of peace to me.

May I float, trusting and supported,
In Your deep, quiet, healing waters.

Goddess of Water, Goddess of flow
Wash through me.
Soothe my pain.
Cleanse my mind.

Let me feel the ebb and flow of emotions,
Allowing them to move through.
Unblock and cleanse that which is stagnant and stuck within me
So that I may feel whole and present and joyful once again.

Whispers from the Elements

FIRE

At Brighid's Forge

As I stand before Your forge
I offer my fears and doubts
To Your sacred fire of transformation.

As I enter the flames
My soul catches fire,
Burning with the divine presence of Your love.

As I step through the other side,
I feel Your alchemy has wrought its magic,
And I rise, newly formed:
Courageous, peaceful, and free.

*

Written in Glastonbury as part of my Priestess training in 2019, after working at Her forge making an iron Goddess spiral.

AIR

I Whisper

I whisper to you on the breeze through leaves,
I sing My love for you through the call of birds.

Feel My presence in the stillness at twilight,
Feel My power in the gale which uproots.

Let My winds blow through the clutter in your mind,
Let My peace come to you with each breath you take.

I will fill you with inspiration and vision,
That you may sing your soul's song with joy.

Whispers from the Elements

GODDESS WITHIN

Inner Space

Vast. Deep. Free.
Oceanic. Limitless.
Infinite love.

This is the space between my breaths ...
The space between my thoughts.

I connect. I drop into this space.
And all is well.

Boundaries melt away. Tension dissolves.
I am supported.
Floating and buoyant on a sea of now.

No beginnings, no endings.
No comparisons.
Just here. Just love.

This space is always within me.

I unlock the door with the key of stillness.

I close my eyes and watch and feel the breath.

Time slows ... My mind expands ... I dissolve.

Pure consciousness expands within me and holds me in Her embrace.

I am alive.
At one.
Spacious.
Free.

I feel You in this space.

We are all here, where nothing divides us.

Whispers from the Soul

Whispers from Mother Earth

Introduction

At the core of your being is a sacred space. A place of deep knowing and wisdom. Timeless. Expansive. Free.

It is your soul.

A place of intuitive understanding, deepest peace, and passionate fire.

An inner voice, which whispers, whose subtle guidance is all too often drowned out by the loud, fretful, analytical mind.

The voice of this inner soul wisdom is knowing and loving. It doesn't shout or judge or cajole.

And your body is the sacred temple which houses your soul.

Where do *you* find your inner portal to this place?

Many will say it is through the heart.

For me, it is through the energies of my heart *and* my womb and the river of energy that flows between them, deep in my body.

So, sink your attention into *your* body.

Whispers from Mother Earth

Take a breath through your heart and see where it wants to take you.

Open your inner eyes and ears and senses.

Maybe you will feel something pulsating, shimmering, expanding... Slowly forming into words or images or feelings.

However it speaks to you, it speaks your truth.

This is your soul's voice.

This is the space through which Mother Earth – the Great Goddess – whispers to you.

Let Her joyful peace and warming fire fill you.

Let Her words bring healing, inspiration and transformation.

Spend time in connection with your soul.

Listen. Listen. Listen.

She has so much to share with you.

Wise and Loving Soul

Your wise and loving soul is quiet and subtle. She doesn't shout or fret or judge.

She never leaves you though you may not always hear her.

But she'll whisper to you when you are ready to listen.

Her words are golden.
Truth. Love. Fire. Wisdom.

They might come as images or feelings.

Open your inner ears and eyes to hear and see.

You will know when the words are coming from your soul because they will feel so true and loving.

The messages may push you, or not quite make sense … but only to your mind.

Your soul will speak through your body as a deep, visceral YES!

And Here I Am

And here I am.
With a heart broken
By confusion, fear, injustice and pain;
Burning with rage and sadness.

And here I am.
With a heart opened
By longing, yearning and seeking
To understand, touch and feel.

And here I am.
With a heart healing
By love flowing in through the cracks:
Soothing, mending, expanding.

And here I am.
Broken open and whole
Held in the embrace of the Beloved
As the divine light shines through.

This Is Life

This is life.
To watch the deepening blue and apricot
Of the sky at dusk.

This is life.
To feel the cool air shivering my skin
As the sun goes down.

This is life.
To notice the first star at twilight
And the moon's silver radiant glow.

This is life.
Feeling my body part of the cool damp evening,
Which warms my heart.

This is life.

My Soul Sings

My soul sings for freedom.
It sings for wild, free, ecstatic dancing,
For flinging limbs whirling through the air and feet stamping in their own time,
For becoming one with the music and merging with the pulse of the universe.

My soul sings for colour.
Vibrant, mismatching hues, celebrating life.
It sings for peacock regality, and for fizzing vivacity, and for warm earthy hues.

My soul sings for beauty.
For the aching perfection of a flower.
For the wild blaze of sunset and the glowing potential of sunrise.
It sings for the magnetic opal moon and for the indigo stillness of a sky full of stars.

My soul sings for the earth,
For the land, the sea and the sky.
And returning to joy through simplicity, stillness and connection.

My soul sings.
It sings for life.
It sings for love.
I sing.

I Remember

Amidst the confusion, doubt and sadness
Something stirs within me and whispers:
I remember.

Through the meanderings of my mind
jumping from one worry to the next,
I feel a calling, and it whispers:
I remember.

Overwhelmed by feeling defeated,
despondent and alone,
A voice rises within me:
I remember.

And I feel an awakening in my heart
And a clarity in my mind.
The confusion fades
My soul expands,
And, yes, I remember!

I remember my soul is made of stars
My heart is the deepest wellspring of love
I come from source and to source I shall return.

I remember that joy is my natural state.
I was not born to suffer; I was born to live!
To embrace this gift of a human life.

Whispers from Mother Earth

I remember the earth is my body
Water is my blood
Air is my breath
And fire is my spirit.

Yes, I remember!
And I choose to rise in love and joy
And shine with radiance and live with freedom in my heart.

Yes, I remember.

The Presence of Love

I breathe once: and acknowledge and honour my body.
I breathe twice: to acknowledge and honour my heart.
I breathe again: to acknowledge and honour the love within me and all around me.

And I sink back to be enfolded and upheld by the divine presence of love.
Eternal. Sacred. Pulsing. Alive.

The divine presence of love within the sunshine and the moonlight.

The divine presence of love in the breeze I feel on my skin and the rustling in the trees' leaves.

The divine presence of love in the stillness and strength of the earth.

The divine presence of love in the depth of the oceans and the flowing of the streams.

The divine presence of love in the sheen on a bird's wing and the scent of a rose and the solidity of a rock.

Eternally present, within me and all around me.
Carrying me. Soothing me. Uplifting me.
Holding me. Healing me.
Awakening me.

The divine presence of love.

And I open my arms,
Root down through my feet,
And lift my face to receive

The divine presence of love,
Which was there in my heart all along.

Oh, Let Me Live!

Oh, let me live from my radiant soul!

Let my soul shine.

Let my heart expand.

Let us shine together in powerful loving harmony.

Rising together as one luminescence which lights up the world.

Whispers from Mother Earth

Come Back To Your Heart

Come back to your heart,
When your mind is racing
And you don't know which way to turn.

Come back to your heart,
When you're lost and lonely
And fear hope will never return.

Come back to your heart,
Even if it feels it's breaking
Through loss and grief and doubt.

Come back to your heart,
If anger blinds you
And you want to stamp and scream and shout.

For in your heart is strength and wisdom
To guide you along the way.

In your heart is love unwavering,
Bringing light to the darkest day.

In your heart is enough kindness and compassion
All fears and doubts to soothe.

In your heart is trust and connection
To help you see the truth.

Whispers from the Soul

Slow down, breathe and quietly listen
To the whispers of your soul.

Telling you that you are love and you are loved,
You are perfect, radiant and whole.

So, come back to your heart,
The centre of love within you,
Whenever you feel alone.

Come back to your heart,
The wellspring of healing within you,
And let Her welcome you home.

Closing Prayer

Whispers from Mother Earth

Our Lady's Prayer

Divine Mother of abundance
Who is within and all around,
Blessed is Your earth, our home.

May we honour and serve You
As You love and support us,
On land, sea and sky.

You provide us all that we need
And love us unconditionally.
Guide us to find love in our hearts for all living beings.

Inspire us to love our bodies and embrace our senses.
As we live in full connection to Your web of life,
Sharing in Your bounty, wisdom and love.

Thank you, forever and ever,
Awen. Awen. Awen.

Blessed be.

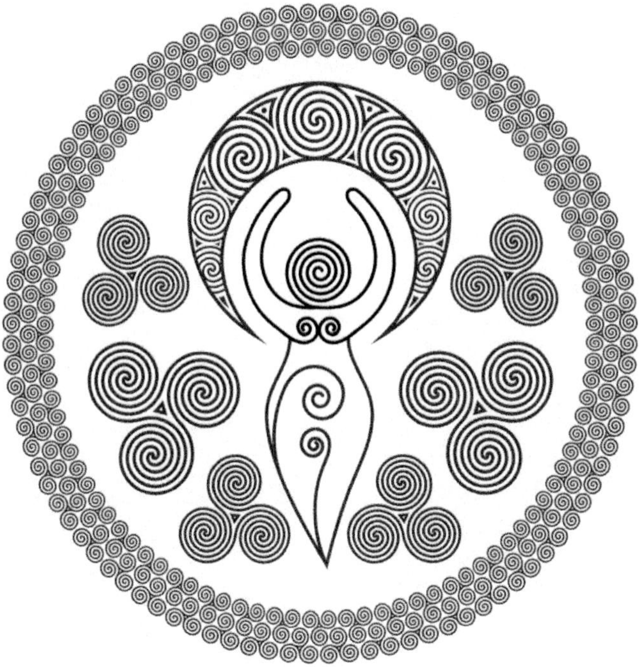

Whispers from Mother Earth

What Next?

Keep in Contact

Be guided to listen to your soul whispers...

Receive my free *Soul Space Restful Nap* meditation + bring some love to your email inbox by signing up for *Soul Wisdom Mail* at: **stellatomlinson.com**

Stay Connected

Website: stellatomlinson.com
Facebook: facebook.com/stellatomlinson
Instagram: @stellasoulwisdom

Spread some whispers across social media: share about this book, or post your pictures of, or inspiration from this book, using the hashtag **#whispersfrommotherearth**

Acknowledgements

I would like to thank and honour my beloved sistars-in-Brighid. The Priestess of Brighde class of 2020! Alison, Amelie, Carol, Darcie, Delphine, Donna, Karan, Lorraine, Luna, Naomi and, never forgetting, Francine and Shannon who completed the first spiral with us. I will be forever grateful for your love, honesty, and sisterhood. May you each radiate Brighid's blessings out into this world in your unique, special ways.

Thank you to Mary Tidbury – you truly were a *Lovely* presence throughout our Priestess training. Your poetry and prayers, your presents and presence were such a profound blessing. When I see an oak tree, I always think of you!

Priestess Marion Brigantia – I am forever grateful I picked up one of your leaflets in the Glastonbury Goddess Temple! Your dedication to Brighid, the way you walk your talk, and your radiant, loving and powerful Queen energy is a constant inspiration to me. Thank you for all that you have taught me – about Brighid, about myself and about life. You truly do bring Her light into this world.

And to my beloved husband Michael, my soul mate, best friend, and biggest champion, thank you for your divine masculine presence in my life. Thank you for holding the space for my flow. For always believing in me when I doubt myself. For loving me, just as I am. And for all the times you've called me to run out into the garden when you've noticed the moon looking radiant in the sky.

About the Author

Stella Tomlinson is a Hampshire (UK)-based author and poet, Priestess and meditation guide who blends the wisdom of nature spirituality with restful dream meditations for healing and creative inspiration.

She wishes to help create a world where the Great Mother and our sacred Earth are held in reverence and love, and where living in alignment with and sensitivity to the sacred cycles of menstruation, the moon and the seasons, and our intuition, have been restored as a natural part of daily life.

Whispers from Mother Earth

As Priestess of Brighid (Goddess of healers, poets & smiths), Stella uses the magic and power of the written and spoken word to bring Brighid's light of healing, inspiration and transformation into the world.

She is author of the book *Peace Lies Within,* regularly writes for her blog, and is creatrix of numerous guided meditations & tool kits.

Stella draws on all that she has studied and practised on her own journey over these last 20 years from the fields of meditation, yoga, energy healing, and Goddess and earth-based nature spirituality. She is a member of the Druid organisation OBOD.

She's been featured on BBC Radio, and her writing has appeared in publications including Kindred Spirit Magazine, The Earth Pathways calendar, OM Yoga & Lifestyle magazine, Elephant Journal and Less Stress London.

Stella is an avid reader and loves walking in nature, taking pictures of sunlight and flowers, gazing at the moon, and visiting Glastonbury and its sacred places as often as possible.

Find out more and connect with Stella at:
stellatomlinson.com